SOUL

SOUL

Poetry to Pluck at your Heartstrings and Inspire your
Inner Core, Written from My Soul to Yours...

KAREN O'LEARY

ISBN: 1516810759
ISBN 13: 9781516810758

Billy Joel eloquently stated, "It's all about soul. It's all about faith and a deeper devotion. It's all about soul..."

As you walk the path that lies ahead of you, may you uncover all of your dreams or, if need be, carve a new path to effect your future.

Soul is identity. Soul is character. Soul is limitless. Soul is powerful. Soul is *you*.

TABLE OF CONTENTS

BREATHE DEEPLY

Outta nowhere,
As piercing as a shot in the night,
I realized…
I was different.

In my head, I had a vision of myself.
But then I listened to the words of others.
I heard their words and their use of descriptors,
But—shockingly and uncomfortably—
Their perceptions did not reflect my vision.

Where was the disconnect?
What was the disconnect?

Define yourself—
But deep down realize only you embody that description.
Because, mostly, the world does not see it right.
It does not judge you right.
It does not see you right.

Outta nowhere,
Like a shot in the night,
It is over.
All they have left are stories to tell—
Their stories,
Their perspectives,
Their incorrect and misguided opinions.

Outta nowhere,
Like the drop of a tiny pin,
You hear it—
The sound of freedom.
Everything that has held you down—
The heavy chains,
The cumbersome weights,
The suffocating words—
Lifted.

From your heart and soul,
The feeling of freedom is purely elating.
The sound of liberty is majestically roaring.

CHANGE OF HEART

Slam! Frustration.
You take over me—
Take hold of me—
Like a pilot, flying a plane
Down, down, and farther down.

Then swoop—
I change the course,
Turning to face the danger.
Slam! Frustration.
You will not take me down today.

IDENTITY

Who are you?

A collective list of adjectives
To slightly scratch the surface:
I am a mother, a wife, a teacher, a daughter,
a sister, an auntie, an athlete, a warrior.

Character found in daily interactions
Epitomizes identity—
Those are the more soulful descriptors.

I am determined, passionate.
I push past limitations.
I push through boundaries—
Further, stronger, limitless.

Who are you?

STUPIDLY SMART

If I am not stupid…
Why is there a large red F on my paper?

If I am not stupid…
Why do I fail every test I take?

If I am not stupid…
Why does everyone know more than me?

If I am not stupid…
Why do I not get what the teacher is saying?

If I am not stupid…
Why do I feel like the world is crashing in on me?

Being stupid is not taking the time to fix the failing grade.
Being stupid is not going to the teacher for extra help.
Being stupid is not trying harder from now on.

Being stupid is comparing myself to everyone else.
Being stupid is thinking that failure defines me.

SMARTY PANTS

What does smart look like?

A pressed white shirt and plaid skirt?
Straight hair and glasses?
A spotless tie, knotted perfectly?
Starched khaki pants and a wool sweater?

What does smart look like?
Because I sure don't want to dress—inappropriately.

LET LIFE

Let what you do shine a light on past, present, and future generations.

Let your positive actions illuminate a path to move you forward.

Let go of the repetitive negative thoughts and influences; they restrain you.

Let your inner soul guide you, and pay no heed to those who make you waiver.

Let the pain in—but only for enough time to resolve it—and move forward.

Let yourself be moved by humanity and strive to reciprocate that feeling to others.

Let your kindness exemplify how humankind should react to the human race.

Let your sense of humor instill a feeling inside others to make their inner cores feel uplifted.

Let your faults be reminders that we are all only human, but striving toward our own definition of perfection.

Let life.

LIFE'S PATH

On the road of life,
There exists both opportunities and chances.

Take the opportunities that are appropriate
To create your own destiny,
But remember there always exists a chance—
A chance to succeed, a chance to fail;
A chance to soar, a chance to lag behind;
A chance to believe, a chance to doubt.

Whatever your position is—
Wherever you are on your path—
Learn from successes and failures.

Look at them as opportunities,
And give yourself a chance to grow.

Give yourself
A chance to think beyond the perimeters,
A chance to change your perception,
A chance to change someone's life.

OWN THIS TOGETHER

Ownership.
It is a concept, seemingly very simple.
Take responsibility for your actions.
Actions will speak louder than words.

My goal, then, is to have my actions
Be so thoughtful and poignant
That they speak volumes—
Actions turned up so loud,
They make your eardrums pound.

Newton's law states that, for every action,
There is an equal and opposite reaction.

Therefore, how I react to someone
Has a ripple effect on how *that* someone
May react to, say, you.

Thus, self-control is a must.
Ownership and thoughtfulness must be
In the forefronts of our minds.
Through our actions and reactions,
We must exemplify actions of positivity,
Because that is the element we want
Reverberating throughout the universe.

Together, we have that much power.

TEACHING IMPRESSIONS

I believe teaching embodies more than a list of traits.
I believe teaching is a way of life.
I believe being a teacher defines you.
I believe teaching is an innate, driving force.

I believe it is divine.

I believe teaching is a calling so loud and piercing,
It cannot—it will not—be ignored.
I believe in humanity, individuality, and creativity.
I believe in cultivating the mind and the spirit.

I know the art of teaching is akin
To placing an ever-so-slight imprint
On a student's heart for eternity.

WHAT DO I STAND FOR AS AN EDUCATOR?

Simple. I stand for humanity.

I stand with those who are trailblazers—
From Martin Luther King Jr. to Rosa Parks.

I stand with those who are courageous—
From Helen Keller to Anne Frank.

I stand with those who provoke curiosity—
From Albert Einstein to William Shakespeare.

I stand with those who empower the future—
From Nelson Mandela to Mahatma Gandhi.

I stand with those who creatively inspire—
From Michelangelo to Pablo Picasso.

I stand with those who strive for harmony—
From Beethoven to John Lennon.

What do I stand for as a teacher?

Simple. I stand for human beings,
From past to present to future generations.

I stand to be inspired.

A NATURAL LOVE

Like the sun's rays—
Too hot to touch—
A parent's love is always
Warm and embracing.

Like the meandering ocean—
Too wide to traverse—
A parent's love is always
Flowing and refreshing.

Like the guiding sky—
Too certain not to follow—
A parent's love is always
An outstretched hand
Providing guidance and inspiration.

Like the air that provides vitality—
Too ubiquitous to contain—
A parent's love is always
Encompassing and breathtaking.

DAWN TO DUSK

With the tears from last night
Covering the glistening earth,
We begin anew.

A rebirth every morning—
A refocus every evening—
To be more accomplished people
Than we reflected in our mirrors the day before.

A rejuvenation every morning—
A renewal every evening—
To be in partnership with our neighbors
To work in concert with each precious individual.

Mother Earth, let us restore our internal character
When our feet touch your tender earth in the morn.
Grant us the strength we require to repair ourselves at dusk,
So we can ambulate proudly the next dawn.

Life is promising and hopeful,
In the manner in which it allows us to begin again,
Every dawn through and to every dusk.

A perfect cyclical motion—
Spinning with grace, around and around—
As we move in harmony with her.

WITH A HEAVY HEART

This is weighing heavy on my heart—
Did I tell you that…
This is weighing heavy on my heart?
Did you know that…
This is weighing heavy on my heart?
Have you heard that…
This is weighing heavy on my heart?
Have I told you that…
This is weighing heavy on my heart?
But I wanted to let you know…

I love you!   I hate you!

That has been weighing
So heavy
On my heart.

CONFLICTED

(A Poem for Two Voices)

This is or isn't what I thought.

What's up?

I'm good.   I'm terrible.

How you doin'?

Fine.   Strugglin'.

One minute I'm up.
The next minute I'm down.

I'm so conflicted.
I feel so restricted, like I can't breathe.

Why is this happenin'?
I shout in my head.

No one can hear me—
They don't care.
I'm just stuck here,
In limbo.
What can I do?
What will I do?

Do you trust me?

Yeah. I do.　　　　　　Nah, man.

Can I help you?

Totally, I'm game.　　　Nah, I'm good.

I'm so conflicted.
I feel so restricted, like I can't breathe.

Why is this happenin'?
I shout in my head.

No one can hear me—
They don't care.
I'm just stuck here,
In limbo.
Frustration builds and builds—
Feel like I'm gonna explode.

I'm so good.　　　　　　I'm so done.

SEARCHING FOR TREASURE

Why was the situation so difficult to see?
A mirror, but ignoring the reflection.
Placid water, but oblivious to its motionless image.
An open book, but unaware of the beautiful story.

Why do we move through the motions—
For so long?

Pretending to be happy,
But yearning for being elated.

Feeling fulfilled,
But constantly looking for enchantment.

Searching for something more—
A lighthouse patrolling the nightly sea—
Bringing to light only the crests of certain waves.

Until one day, with limitless eyes viewing your world,
The pieces become clear, evident.
A dusty treasure map has been exposed.
The next step in your journey is in your control.

The individual, undiscovered path will not limit.
Go discover, with each step, uncovering true greatness.

TINY HANDS

The juxtaposition of your tiny fingers in the palm of my hand
Feels like the brightest shining star in all of the universe
Aglow in the sky.

You are my guide.
I follow your lead.
Show me the world through your eyes.

When I perceive the world this way,
My curiosity is elevated to new heights.

Feelings of innocence and newness
Engulf my being, flowing over me like an ocean wave.

You are my guide.
I follow your lead.
Show me the world through your eyes.

ODE TO SOUL CYCLE

Roosters—the best way to start your day—
Positive motivation with a pack mentality,
Working as a united front,
A force of positivity with each push,
We propel forward.

Clip in your shoes, and prepare for melodious chaos.
Mental focus is fundamental.
Physical insecurity is happening.
Staying present in the moment, in the zone—
Never to anticipate, always to participate.
Work together with the soul community,
Achieving milestones, breaking boundaries,
Shredding through words that bind us.

Soul is a mentality.
It is a way of life.
It is the only way worth living.
Let your soul breathe.
Let your soul guide.
Let your soul transcend the impossible.

LIVE, LOVE, BE TOGETHER

As you embark upon your life of love…

Feel the support surrounding you, for it will never waiver.
Savor the utter joy you feel today; may it last you a lifetime.
Laugh aloud.

Share your love for each other; it will strengthen your spirit.
Support each other through the difficult times; it will tighten your bond.
Encourage your wildest dreams.
Smile often.

Take time to listen to each other; this is the secret to respect.
Admire one another's ambitions; let them propel you forward.
In times of change, revert back to the basics.
Love brought you together.

Trust your hearts; pure happiness is precious.
Love completely today, tomorrow, and always.

happy forever after

Love is an endless circle of trust, lasting unison Marriage is a delicate harmonious dance performed together in honesty, sharing, caring, laughter and

FORWARD PROGRESSION

Try to predict an outcome,
Try to foresee tomorrow
Or the days that will come—
Not to be done.

Rather achieve greatness every day.
Accept challenges, because they are life's lessons.

Eventually,
Everything will fall into place.

Be wise enough to gaze back at your steps—
Revelation of the larger picture in your sight;
At that point, you will realize your great achievements
And continue to move forward.

A REMARKABLE MAN

His smile could light up the darkest night.
His embrace could make a granddaughter feel like
The only person in the world.
His wit and charm, his caring heart,
His unwavering demeanor, seem to exude comfort in his presence—
His wisdom and experience, notably his enthusiasm about life,
Remarkable and worthy of emulating.

Whether a long engagement or a brief encounter,
A life is forever changed.
A heart—rather, two hearts grow bigger,
Beat faster and stronger because of it.

A WISH FOR TWO...

Strength on difficult days.
Smiles when sadness interferes.
Confidence to reassure your doubts.
Laughter to lift your spirits.

Friendships to fulfill your beings.
Beauty for you both to gaze upon.
Happiness to warm your hearts.
Patience to listen to one another.

And a lifetime of unconditional love.

Made in the USA
Middletown, DE
03 October 2015